POCKET IRISH PHRASE BOOK

Paul Dorris

Appletree Press

First published and printed by
The Appletree Press Ltd
7 James Street South
Belfast BT2 8DL
1983

Text by Paul Dorris
Edited and designed by Appletree Press Ltd

British Library Cataloguing in Publication Data

Dorris, Paul
  Pocket Irish phrase book.
  1. Irish language-Conservation and phrase
    book
  I. Title
  491.6'283'421   PB1227

  ISBN 0-86281-010-8

Éire

The areas where Irish is regularly spoken are known as **An Ghaeltacht** and are shown by black shading.

Notes

In the pronunciation guides the symbol *I* is used to represent the sounds of the Irish *ái* (or *agh* in certain words) and should not be confused with 'l'. For example:

face	**aghaidh**
	lee
place	**ait**
	Itch

In the translations in this book, the English is set in Roman type, the Irish in bold type, and the guides to pronunciation in italic. For example:

the little window   **an fhuinneog bheag**
in inyog vug

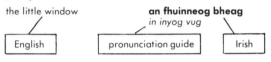

| English | pronunciation guide | Irish |

Contents

Introduction

The purpose of this book is to acquaint visitors, or indeed anyone else with little or no knowledge of Irish, with some of the more common words and phrases currently in use in the language. There is also a brief description of Irish grammar, and this should enable the reader to expand on the phrases given by substituting nouns, persons, adjectives etc. Irish grammar is a difficult subject and a full description of it is outside the scope of this book. The concise description given here, however, should not be off-putting but a useful guide to the reader who wishes to use the phrases given with a greater degree of confidence and accuracy. The aim has been to provide a basis for simple conversation in Irish and to encourage the reader to proceed further on his or her own account and acquire some fluency in the language. The best, if not the only, way to learn a language well is to hear it spoken in its natural setting, and this book may provide an incentive to do just that. Anyone interested in taking the subject a stage further will find numerous books, grammars, dictionaries, etc. easily available, as well as a good selection of tapes, records and other aids. One finds, however, that the average Irish-speaker is the best source of assistance and this is where it is important to be able to ask the right questions.

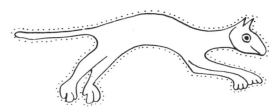

Historical Background

Irish and her sister languages, Welsh and Breton, are among the oldest living languages in Europe. Written records go back to the early Christian period when Latin was often the usual written medium. Irish scribes would sometimes 'gloss' or annotate in the margins of their manuscripts, and it is from these glosses that much of our knowledge of 'Old Irish' has come. Another form of early writing was 'Ogham', consisting of a code of strokes and dots representing the letters, and usually incribed on the edges of upright stones. Hundreds of these 'Ogham Stones' still survive and they usually contain the name of a person, probably as a memorial. They were sometimes erected in honour of dead chieftains or warriors.

Irish developed from one of the Celtic dialects brought to bronze age Ireland and Britain by the iron age Celts, who inhabited Central Europe some three thousand years ago. Ireland was invaded many times and factual evidence is sometimes difficult to obtain. The oral tradition, however, refers consistently to specific events such as 'The Great Plague' and 'The Great Flood' etc. in very factual terms, along-side obviously myth-ological events. Quite often the claims of 'folk history' are corroborated by documentary and other evidence. The invaders of the pre-Celtic period such as Parthalon, Tuatha Dé Danann, Fir Bolg, Milesians, Picts (or Cruithni) are all considered as being ancient inhabitants of Ireland. It can be assumed that when the Celts eventually succeeded in conquering the country that it was a land of many diverse languages, cultures and peoples, even though the population must have been small, and these pre-Celtic languages are thought to have had some influence on what we now call Irish.

Irish was first called 'Gaelic' or 'Goidelic' ('Gaeilge' is the Irish word for the language) by the Welsh. Gaelic mythology and folklore abounds in typically Celtic themes and motifs, such as 'dícheannú' (beheading one's slain enemy) or the 'curadhmhír' (the champion's portion at the feast), as well as many others. Some months of the year are named after pagan Celtic dieties: 'Lúnasa', the month of August, after the god Lugh, as is the town of Lyons in France. There are, of course, hundreds of Irish place-names with Celtic/pagan origins.

The Viking invasions between the eighth and tenth centuries left lasting traces on the culture and language of the population, and many typically Scandinavian words are found in modern Irish, in particular those relating to ships and navigation. The next settlers, the Normans in the twelfth century, brought about a strong French influence, in particular on the literature of the period. Some of the southern dialects of Irish are still detectably influenced by Norman French, and contain several typically French words like 'garsún' (boy).

In the seventeenth century, under English rule, many Irish chieftains and teachers were forced either to emigrate or go into hiding, and for many people education continued only in the illegal 'hedge schools', in fields, barns and sheds. This led to the curious situation where a landlord would address a tenant in English, only to be answered in Greek or Latin. When the first ordnance survey team arrived in Ireland in the early nineteenth century to map the country it enlisted the help of local people, and this team established the anglicised versions of place-names which are in use to-day.

It was also at the beginning of the nineteenth century that scholars, notably Germans, began to unravel the mysteries of 'Old Irish' and Irish studies became a recognized scholarly pursuit. Towards the end of the century the Irish cultural revolution, or 'renaissance', began. Conradh na Gaeilge (The Gaelic League) was founded in 1893 with the principle aim of reviving the Irish language, which was showing signs of decline. There are branches of the Conradh in most towns and these provide excellent classes in Irish at all levels. It is possible that it was only constant pressure from and perseverance of this group that prevented the complete loss of Irish in both the Gaeltacht and in the country as a whole. One of the successes of Conradh na Gaeilge has been the re-establishment of Irish writing as an artistic medium. For about a century Irish writing has been on the increase and the short story has emerged as the medium *par excellence* of this literature. There is also a wide selection of journals, newspapers and magazines available and these are of considerable benefit to learners of the language as well as being a useful vehicle for writers of all types.

Who speaks Irish and where?

The Republic of Ireland, or Eire, is officially a bilingual state with Irish and English having equal status under the law. No-one knows for certain the exact number of Irish-speakers but interest in the language is perhaps as strong now as it has ever been.

The districts in which Irish is still spoken habitually are known as 'An Ghaeltacht' and these are mainly situated on the west coast i.e. in Donegal where 'Ulster Irish' (U), is spoken, in Galway and north Mayo where 'Connacht Irish' (C), is spoken, and in parts of Cork, Kerry and Waterford where 'Munster Irish' (M) is the usual dialect. The Irish used in this book is a composite of the main dialects, based on the so-called 'standard' or official form, the intention being to achieve intelligibility in any part of the country. Regional variations are occasionally given, followed by U, M or C to indicate the dialect concerned or the province in which the variation is normally used.

Pronunciation

The system of pronunciation given in this book is based on normal English spelling. It is impossible to give the exact pronunciation by this method but it does have the advantage of being both simple and intelligible. No attempt should be made to stress the words or syllables in a phrase as stresses and accents vary widely throughout the country. The best method is to speak the words, using the anglicised pronunciation; using this 'neutral' accent you are less likely to go astray. As well as the transliterations, a literal translation is given with some of the phrases and these are indicated by the abbreviation 'Lit.'.

When *t* is followed or preceded by one of the slender vowels *e* or *i* it is usually pronounced like English *ch* as in *chip*. The word *te* (hot), for example, is pronounced *cheh*. When *t* is followed or preceded by one of the broad vowels *a, o* or *u* it is pronounced like English *t* (as in *tea*). The tip of the tongue is placed behind the upper front teeth for this sound. When *t* is aspirated, i.e. *th*, it is pronounced like English *h* when it occurs at the beginning of a word, e.g. **mo theach**, *mu hakh* (my house). If it occurs at the end of a word it is always silent, e.g. **fáth** *fa* (a reason) or has an 'h' sound.

The letter *c* in Irish is pronounced like English *k*, e.g. **carr** *kar* (a car). When it is followed by a slender vowel however, (*i* or *e*), it acquires a *ky* sound as in **cearr**, *kyar* (wrong). The sound *ch* is very common in Irish and can sometimes be a source of difficulty for the learner. It is, in fact, a common sound in many languages and can be pronounced like the *ch* in 'Bach' or Scottish 'loch', or like the *gh* in 'lough'. At the end of a word it is sometimes pronounced like a very strong *h* or *hh* as in **teach**, *chakh* or *chahh* (house).

The letter *d* in Irish, when used with a slender vowel, sounds like English *j* e.g. **deoch**, *jukh* (drink), or **díon**, *jeen* (roof). When used with a broad vowel it can be pronounced like English *d*, e.g. **doras**, *darass* (door). When *d* becomes aspirated, i.e. *dh* it sounds like *y*, e.g. **mo dheoch**, *mu yukh* (my drink). When *dh* is used with a broad vowel it sounds approximately like English *g*, but with a slightly 'breathy' quality: **mo dhoras**, *mu garass* (my door).

Sometimes the vowels in Irish are short and sometimes long. The vowel *a*, when short, can be pronounced like English *a* as in 'bat', but when long (*á*) it is pronounced like *aw* or *au* in most dialects. In Ulster it is more like the long *a* in English 'park'.

The vowel *o* is similar to English *u*: **dona**, *dunna* (bad). When the *o* is long (*ó*) it can be represented by *au*, as in **bó**, *bau* (cow).

The vowel *u* is not unlike the English *u* when short, but when long (*ú*) it is pronounced like the English *oo*: **gúna**, *goona* (a dress).

The vowel *e* has several values and many of these will become apparent from the pronunciations given with the phrases. When *e* is long (*é*) it is usually like *ay*: **féar**, *fayer* (grass).

The vowel *i* is like its equivalent in English: **mill**, *mill* (to destroy). If the *i* is long (*í*) it is pronounced like the English *ee*: **sín**, *sheen* (stretch). The symbol I represents the *i* in English words like 'fire', 'spire', 'shine', etc., and it is used to express the sounds of the Irish *ái* or *agh* in certain words: **aghaidh**, *Iee* (a face); **ait**, *Itch* (a place).

Generally, consonants with slender vowels should be spoken with the lips quite close together as in **bean**, *ban* (a woman), **fear**, *far* (a man), **peann**, *pan* (a pen). Consonants with broad vowels (*a, o, u,*) are pronounced with much more rounded lips: **bán**, *bawn* (white), **fada**, *fawda* (long), **punt**, *punt* (a pound).

The digraph *ao* must be given special considera-
tion, as in some parts of the country it comprises a
sound which cannot be readily described in English
phonetics. It is sometimes pronounced like English
ee and sometimes like *ay*, as in **saol**, *seel* or *sayl*
(life). Either of these pronunciations is acceptable.

The consonants *l*, *n* and *r* vary considerably
according to whether they are used with broad or
slender vowels or whether they are single or
double; *l* with a slender vowel is pronounced like
the *l* in English 'bottle'; *l* at the beginning of a word
is pronounced with a *y* sound when followed by a
slender vowel: **liom**, *lyum* (with me), **leat**, *lyat* (with
you); *ll* has a more rounded sound similar to the *ll* in
'brilliant'. The *n* is quite similar to the English *n*
except when it is doubled, *nn*; this sound sometimes
has a nasal quality. When the double consonant is
followed by *e*, or *i*, it acquires a *y* sound: **fáinne**,
fawnya (a ring). When *nn* occurs at the end of a
word it can sometimes have a slight *ng* sound:
binn, *bing* (harmonious). This is a subtle sound and
is only prominent in certain parts of the country.

Both *r* and *rr* are not unlike their English counter-
parts, but there are some differences. *ir* is a most
unusual sound to the ears of most English speakers,
but is easily mastered with a little practice.

The consonant *g* is like English *g*, but when
aspirated it is unlike any sound in English; *gh* is like
a 'breathy' version of *g*, the *h* being quite
noticeable.

The consonants *b*, *m* and *p* change completely when aspirated: *p* becomes *ph*, which sounds exactly like English *f*; *bh* sounds like *v* when followed or preceded by a slender vowel (*e* or *i*). It becomes a *w* sound when it has *a*, *o*, or *u* before or after it; *abh*, *obh*, and *ubh* are pronounced: *aw*, *ow* and *uw* respectively. In some southern dialects the *w* sound may be replaced by *v*. There is considerable regional variation in this respect. When *m* is aspirated (*mh*) it also sounds like *w* or *v*, depending on whether it has a broad or slender consonant alongside it, and is exactly like *b* in this respect.

Grammar

The following notes explain certain points arising from the phrases, while other grammatical points are dealt with as they arise in the text.

Nouns

Nouns in Irish are either masculine or feminine. Here are a few examples of masculine nouns with the article:

the man	**an fear**
	a far
the door	**an doras**
	a darass
the book	**an leabhar**
	a lyower
the floor	**an t-urlár**
	a turlar

Note the use of *t* in front of a vowel: **urlár** (a floor).
Also that the *n* is sometimes dropped in everyday
speech:

the clock	**an clog**
	a klug
the watch	**an t-uaireadóir**
	a toorador
the cupboard	**an cófra**
	a kofra
the boy	**an buachaill**
	a bookhil
the house	**an teach**
	a chakh
the time	**an t-am**
	an tam
the aeroplane	**an t-eitleán**
	an tetchalan

Now here are a few feminine words:

the woman	**an bhean**
	in van
	(but **bean**: a woman)
the window	**an fhuinneog**
	in inyog (*fh* is silent)
the river	**an abhainn**
	in owan

In the case of feminine nouns beginning with a
vowel there is no *t* after the article *an*.

the hour	**an uair**
	in oor
the weather	**an aimsir**
	in Imsher
the shoe	**an bhróg**
	a vrog
the hand	**an lámh**
	a lauw or *lawv* (C, M)

Feminine words beginning with *s* have a *t* placed in
front of them when used with *an*, as in:

the week	**an tseachtain**
	a chakhtan
the street	**an tsráid**
	a trlj

Adjectives

The adjective always follows the noun which it describes:

the big house	**an teach mór**
	inchakh more
the long road	**an bóthar fada**
	in bohar fada
(a) nice town	**baile deas**
	bala jass
(a) little dog	**madra beag**
	madra bug (C, M)
	(In Ulster the word
	madadh, *madoo*, is
	used for dog)

Notice that the indefinite article 'a' does not exist in Irish.

If a word is feminine, like those listed above, then the adjective following it is sometimes aspirated (The Irish word for this is **séimhiú**, *shevoo*, to soften.) This process is also referred to as lenition and is a characteristic of the Celtic languages. Here are some examples of adjectives with feminine nouns:

(a) big woman	**bean mhór**
	ban wore
the big woman	**an bhean mhór**
	in van wore
fine (good) weather	**aimsir mhaith**
	Imsher woih
the little window	**an fhuinneog bheag**
	in inyog vug
(a) big window	**fuinneog mhór**
	fwinyog wore

Here are some more adjectives:

pretty	**dóighiúil**
	doyooil
ugly	**gránna**
	grawna
short	**gairid**
	gurij
fat	**ramhar**
	rawar

thin	**tanaí**
	tanee
high	**ard**
	ard
low	**íseal**
	eeshal
full	**lán**
	lawn
empty	**folamh**
	fuloo
bright	**geal**
	gyal
white	**bán**
	bawn
black	**dubh**
	doo (U), *duv* (C, M)
blue	**gorm**
	gurim
green	**glas**
	glass
yellow	**buí**
	bwee
red	**dearg**
	jareg
red (of hair), ginger	**rua**
	rooa
grey	**liath**
	leea
brown	**donn**
	dun

Prepositions

Irish can be described as a language of prepositions, as opposed to a language like English which is largely 'verbal' by comparison. When a preposition is used with a verb it can totally change the meaning of that verb, or give the verb a new shade of meaning. Irish speakers will often use a preposition and verb phrase in place of a simple verb, e.g. **tá sé ag teacht** he is coming (*taw shay a chakht*), but when a preposition such as *le*, (with) is used then the phrase can have a different meaning entirely (**leat**, pronounced *lyat*, means literally 'with you'):

| he agrees with you | **tá sé ag teacht leat** |

This can also mean 'he is coming with you'. This type of phrase is extremely common. In the above example the verb **aontaigh** (to agree), could have been used.

   Some prepositions cause aspiration or eclipsis of following nouns (eclipsis is more common in the south and aspiration in the north, but in many cases either can be used, the various dialects differing considerably in this respect:

on the wall	**ar an bhalla** *air a walla* (U)
on the wall	**ar an mballa** *air a malla* (C, M)

Both of these are equally correct and can of course be used anywhere by the learner. Likewise 'c' is eclipsed by g = gc; 'd' by 'n' = nd; 'f' by 'bh' = bhf; 'g' by n = ng; 'p' by b = bp; and 't' by d = dt. In each case the eclipsing consonant is the one pronounced.

in the bottle	**sa bhuidéal** *sa wujell*
through the window	**tríd an fhuinneog** *treej in inyog*
with the man	**leis an fhear** *lesh in yar*
under the cup	**faoin chupán** *fween khupan*
with the woman	**leis an bhean** *lesh in van*
at the door	**ag an doras** *eg a darass*
on the ground	**ar an talamh** *air a taloo*
past the house	**thar an teach** *har a chakh*
under the chair	**faoin chathaoir** *fween khaheer*
in my pocket	**i mo phóca** *i mu foca*
come from the fire	**tar ón tine** *tar owin chinee*

Here is a list of prepositions:

at	**ag**
	eg
out (of)	**as**
	iss
towards/to	**chuig**
	hig
from/off/of	**de**
	de
to/for	**do**
	dau
along with	**fara**
	farra
under	**faoi**
	fwee
between	**idir**
	idder
in	**i**
	i (as in 'hid')
with	**le**
	le
on	**ar**
	air
before	**roimh**
	riv
past	**thar**
	har
through	**trí**
	tree
from	**ó**
	o (as in 'bone')
round about	**um**
	umm

These prepositions do not always have an exact English equivalent. They are more often found in combination with the personal pronouns (you, me, her, etc.) and the more important of these will be encountered later. Here is an example:

before	**roimh**
	riv
before me	**romham**
	rowam
before you	**romhat**
	rowat

before him/it	**roimhe**
	riva
before her/it	**roimpi**
	rimpee
before us	**romhainn**
	roween
before you (pl.)	**romhaibh**
	rowiv
before them	**rompu**
	rumpoo

Here is another important one:

on	**ar**
	air
on me	**orm**
	urram
on you	**ort**
	urt
on him/it	**air**
	air
on her/it	**uirthi**
	urhee
on us	**orainn**
	ureen
on you (pl.)	**oraibh**
	uriv
on them	**orthu**
	urhoo

It can be seen from this that the endings for the prepositional pronouns form fairly regular patterns.

Plurals

There are several ways of forming plurals in Irish, despite attempts at standardization and, daunting though it may sound, it is probably best to learn each plural as it arises. The method of forming plurals often varies from district to district but this should not be a problem as the root-word generally remains recognizable. Here are a few common examples:

the men	**na fir**
	na fir

the women	**na mná**
	na m-naw (C, M),
	na mra (U)
a person	**duine**
	dinna
the people	**na daoine**
	na deenee
the houses	**na tithe**
	na teeha
a tree	**crann**
	kran
the trees	**na crainn**
	na krin
a light	**solas**
	sulass
the lights	**na solais**
	na sulish
a river	**abhainn**
	owen
the rivers	**na haibhneacha**
	na hivnakha

(Note that the article 'the' changes from '*an*' to '*na*' in the nominative plural.)

Personal pronouns

I	**mé**
	may
you	**tú**
	too
he	**sé**
	shay
she	**sí**
	shee
we	**muid**
	mij
you (pl.)	**sibh**
	shiv
they	**siad**
	sheead

These are sometimes used with their emphatic or strong form. This is given in brackets. All nouns in Irish can have this emphatic form under certain circumstances, e.g. expression of ownership.

me	**mé, (mise)**
	may, (misha)
you	**tú, (tusa)**
	hoo, (tussa)
him	**é, (eisean)**
	ay, (eshan)
her	**í, (ise)**
	ee, (isha)
us	**muid, (muidinne)**
	muj, (mujinya)
you (pl.)	**sibh, (sibhse)**
	shiv, (shivsha)
them	**iad, (iadsan)**
	eead, (eeadsan)

When used with a verb (for example **tá**, to be) personal pronouns in the nominative case are as follows:

I am	**tá mé**
	taw may
you are	**tá tú**
	taw too
he/it is	**tá sé**
	taw shay
she/it is	**tá sí**
	taw shee
we are	**táimid**
	tawmij
you (pl.) are	**tá sibh**
	taw shiv
they are	**tá siad**
	taw sheead

Verbs

The verb **tá** (to be) is used to express a state or condition, but the verb **is** (to be), pronounced *iss*, must be used when expressing existence and with certain other concepts, e.g.:

he is big	**tá sé mór**
	taw shay more
he is here	**tá sé anseo**
	taw shay inshaw
he is a man	**is fear é**
	iss far ay
he is a big man	**is fear mór é**
	iss far more ay

Is is used in many other structures as well e.g. **is maith liom é** (I like it). The distinction between **is** and **tá** must be closely observed. Many learners of Irish sometimes say, for example, **tá sé teach** for 'it is a house'. The structure **tá sé teach** does not exist in Irish. One can, however, say **tá sé ina theach**, literally 'it is in its state of being a house'.

Is, in conjunction with **le**, is used to express ownership, e.g. **is liom é** (it is mine). This literally means, 'it is with me'.

the coat is yours	**is leat an cóta**
	iss lyat in kota
the money is ours	**is linn an t-airgead**
	iss linn in tarigad
the bicycle is his	**is leis an rothar**
	iss leis in ruhar
they own the place	**is leo an áit**
	iss law in itch
they are yours (pl.)	**is libh iad**
	iss liv eead
the shoes are hers	**is léi na bróga**
	iss leyh na brauga
the house is John's	**is le Seán an teach**
	iss le shan in chakh
who owns the book?	**cé leis an leabhar?**
	kay lesh in lyower
it isn't mine	**ní liom é**
	nee lyum ay
is this your hat?	**an leat an hata seo?**
	un lyat in hata shaw
no (it is not)	**ní liom**
	nee lyum
yes (it is)	**is liom**
	iss lyum

The negative of **is** is **ní**, and the interrogative, or question form, is **an**:

is it a glass?	**an gloine é?**
	in glinya ay
yes (it is)	**is ea**
	sha
no (it is not)	**ní hea**
	nee ha

Fortunately, there are few irregular verbs in Irish and these also happen to be the most commonly used of all the verbs. They are as follows:

make (or do)	**déan**
	jan
come	**tar**
	tar
hear	**clois**
	klish
see	**feic**
	feck
go	**téigh**
	chey
give	**tabhair**
	towar
get	**faigh**
	fi
say	**abair**
	abber
take, (bear, bring or give birth)	**beir**
	beyr
to eat	**ith**
	ih

Most of these verbs will be encountered again later in the book, as will the other points mentioned in this section. One point to bear in mind about the irregular verbs is that they nearly all have dependant forms. These are used in asking questions, in the negative and in reported speech. Here, for example, is the verb **tá** in the present, past, future, conditional and habitual tenses, using the personal pronoun **mé**. Any of the other personal pronouns could be used instead. There are several other tenses in Irish, but these are less likely to be encountered:

I am	**tá mé** (U), **táim** (C, M)
	taw may (U), *tawim* (C, M)
I will be	**beidh mé**
	bay may
I was	**bhí mé**
	vee may

(Note: **tá** is the present tense form of the substantive verb **bí**. **Tá mé anseo** = I am here (now); **bím**

anseo = I am (usually) here.)

I am	**bím** *beem*
I am not	**níl mé** *neeil may*
I will not be	**ní bheidh mé** *nee vay may*
I was not	**ní raibh mé** *nee row may*
I would not be	**ní bheinn** *nee veyeen*
I am not	**ní bhím** *nee veem*
am I?	**an bhfuil mé** *un will may*
will I be?	**an mbeidh mé** *un may may*
would I be?	**an mbeinn?** *un mayeen*
am I?	**an mbím** *un meem*
was I?	**an raibh mé?** *un row may*

Reported speech is simply saying what someone else said:

he said that...	**dúirt sé go...** *dooart shay gu...*
he said that he was ill	**dúirt sé go raibh sé tinn** *dooart shay gu row shay chin*

or with **deir** (to say):

he says that...	**deir sé go...** *jer shay gu...*
he says that he will be here	**deir sé go mbeidh sé anseo** *jer shay gu may shay un-shaw*

and in a negative form:

he says that I was not in the house	**deir sé nach raibh mé sa teach** *jer shay nakh row may sa chakh*

Numbers

Numerals in Irish are as follows:

one	**aon**
	ayn
two	**dó**
	dau
three	**trí**
	tree
four	**ceathair**
	kehar
five	**cúig**
	kooig
six	**sé**
	shay
seven	**seacht**
	shakht
eight	**ocht**
	okht
nine	**naoi**
	nee
ten	**deich**
	jeykh
eleven	**aon déag**
	aynjeg
twelve	**dó dhéag**
	dauyeg
thirteen	**trí déag**
	treejeg
fourteen	**ceathair déag**
	keharjeg
fifteen	**cúig deag**
	kooigjeg
sixteen	**sé déag**
	shayjeg
seventeen	**seacht déag**
	shakhtjeg
eighteen	**ocht déag**
	okhtjeg
nineteen	**naoi déag**
	neejeg
twenty	**fiche**
	fiha
thirty	**tríocha**
	treeakha

forty	**daichead**
	dIhad
fifty	**caoga**
	kayga
sixty	**seasca**
	shaska
seventy	**seachtó**
	shakhto
eighty	**ochtó**
	okhto
ninety	**nócha**
	nokha
one hundred	**céad**
	keyd

When used adjectivally, some of these numbers differ slightly. There are several counting systems in Irish, although the following is the simplest and best known:

one pound	**punt amháin**
	punt awoin
two pounds	**dhá phunt**
	dau funt
three pounds	**trí phunt**
	tree funt
four pounds	**ceithre phunt**
	kerra funt
five pounds	**cúig phunt**
	kooig funt
six pounds	**sé phunt**
	shay funt
seven pounds	**seacht bpunt**
	shakht bunt
eight pounds	**ocht bpunt**
	okht bunt
nine pounds	**naoi bpunt**
	nee bunt
ten pounds	**deich bpunt**
	jeykh bpunt
eleven pounds	**punt déag**
	punt jeg
twelve pounds	**dhá phunt déag**
	dau funt jeg
thirteen pounds	**trí phunt déag**
	tree funt jeg

fourteen pounds	**ceithre phunt déag**
	kerra funt jeg
fifteen pounds	**cúig phunt déag**
	kooig funt jeg
sixteen pounds	**sé phunt déag**
	shay funt jeg
seventeen pounds	**seacht pbunt déag**
	shakht bunt jeg
eighteen pounds	**ocht bpunt déag**
	okht bunt jeg
nineteen pounds	**naoi bpunt déag**
	nee bunt jeg
twenty pounds	**fiche punt**
	fiha punt
twenty-one pounds	**punt is fiche**
	punt iss fiha
twenty-two pounds	**dhá phunt is fiche**
	gau funt iss fiha
thirty pounds	**tríocha punt**
	treeakha punt
forty pounds	**daichead punt**
	dlhad punt

Counting people is slightly different yet again:

one person	**duine amháin**
	dinna awoin
one man	**fear amháin**
	far awoin
one girl	**cailín amháin**
	kalleen awoin
two people	**beirt**
	berch
two men	**beirt fhear**
	berch ar
three people	**triúr**
	troor
three women	**triúr ban**
	troor ban
four people	**ceathrar**
	kehrar
four boys	**ceathrar gasúr**
	kehrar gasoor
five people	**cúigear**
	kooigar

five men	**cúigear fear**
	kooigar far
six people	**seisear**
	sheshar
six women	**seisear ban**
	sheshar ban
seven people	**seachtar**
	shakhtar
seven children	**seachtar páiste**
	shakhtar pashtee
eight people	**ochtar**
	okhtar
eight fools	**ochtar amadán**
	okhtar amadaun
nine people	**naonúr**
	neenoor
nine sailors	**naonúr mairnéalach**
	neenoor marnyalakh
ten people	**deichniúr**
	jeynoor
eleven people	**duine déag**
	dinna jeg
twelve people	**beirt déag**
	berch jeg

Common Words and Phrases

how are you?	**cad é mar atá tú?**
	kajay mara ta too (U)
how are you?	**cén chaoi a bhfuil tú?**
	keng khee awill too (C)
how are you?	**conas tá tú?**
	kunas taw too (M)
I'm fine, thanks	**tá go maith, go raibh maith agat**
	taw gu mah, gura mah ugut
good-bye	**slán leat** (if you are staying)
	slawn lyat
good-bye	**slán agat** (if you are leaving)
	slawn ugut
good-day, hello	**Dia duit**
	jeea ditch

the reply to this is:	**Dia's Muire duit** *jeeass mwurra ditch*
goodnight	**oíche mhaith** *eeha wah*
what time is it?	**cad é an t-am?** *kajay un tam*
it is five o'clock	**tá sé a cúig a chlog** *taw shay a kooig a khlug*
big	**mór** *more*
small	**beag** *bug*
hot	**te** *cheh*
cold	**fuar** *fooar*
bigger	**níos mó** *neess mow*
smaller	**níos lú** *neess loo*
hotter	**níos teo** *neess chaw*
colder	**níos fuaire** *neess fooara*
hot water	**uisce te** *ishka cheh*
cold water	**uisce fooar** *ishka fooar*
I am hungry	**tá ocras orm** *taw ukrass uram*
I am thirsty	**tá tart orm** *taw tart uram*
it is cold today	**tá sé fuar inniu** *taw shay fooar inyoo*
it is very warm	**tá sé an-te** *taw shay ann-cheh*
the weather is fine	**tá an aimsir go maith** *taw un Imsher gu mah*
it is cold today	**tá sé fuar inniu** *taw shay fooar inyoo*
isn't it a nice day?	**nach deas an lá é inniu?** *nakh jass un law ay inyoo*
I like weather like this	**is maith liom aimsir mar seo** *iss mah lyum Imsher mar shaw*

do you like tea?	**an maith leat tae?**
	un mah lyat tay
yes, I do	**is maith**
	iss mah
no, I do not	**ní maith**
	nee mah
do you take sugar?	**an ólann tú siúcra?**
	un awlan too shookra
are you hungry?	**an bhfuil ocras ort?**
	un will ukrass urt
yes (I am hungry)	**tá**
	taw
no	**níl**
	neel
are you warm enough?	**an bhfuil tú te go leor?**
	in will too cheh go lyowr
where are we now?	**cá bhfuilimid anois?**
	ka willimij anish
what is that?	**cad é sin?**
	kajay shin
where is it?	**cá bhfuil sé?**
	ka will shay
how do you say?	**cad é mar déarfá?**
	kajay mar jerrha
what is your name?	**cad is ainm duit?**
	kad iss anyim ditch
my name is...	**...is ainm dom**
	...iss anyim dum
switch on the light	**las an solas**
	lass un suliss
put out the light	**cuir as an solas**
	kur iss un suliss
switch on the television	**cuir suas an teilifís**
	kur sooas un tellefish
excuse me	**gabh mo leithscéal**
	gow mu layskal
don't mention it	**ná habhair é**
	naw habber ay
would you like a drink?	**ar mhaith leat deoch?**
	air way lyat jokh
yes (I would)	**ba mhaith**
	ba woy
it does not matter	**is cuma**
	iss kumma
it does not matter to me	**is cuma liom**
	iss kumma lyum

I'm glad to see you	**tá athas orm thú a fheiceáil** *taw ahass uram hoo eck-al*
don't worry	**ná bí buartha** *haw bee boorha*
I feel ill	**mothaím tinn** *muheeam chinn*
I have a cold	**tá slaghdán orm** *taw slaydan uram*
would you like more tea?	**ar mhaith leat tuilleadh tae?** *air woy lyat chilloo tay*
can you drive?	**an féidir leat tiomáint?** *in fayjar lyat chuminch*
everyone	**gach duine** *gak dinna*
everywhere	**gach áit** *gak itch*
almost	**beagnach** *bugnach*
much/many	**a lán/cuid mhór** *a lann/kuj wore*
how many/much?	**cá mhéad** *ka vayd*
somebody	**duine éigin** *dinna aygin*
why (is that)?	**cad chuige (sin)?** *ka tiga (shin)*
turn left here	**gabh ar chlé anseo** *gow air khlay unshaw*
turn right there	**gabh ar dheis ansin** *gow air yaysh unshin*
do you speak Irish?	**an bhfuil Gaeilge agat?** *un will gaylga ugut*
What is your name?	**Cad é an t-ainm atá ort?** *kajay in tanyim ataw urt*
My name is Nora	**Nóra atá orm** *nora ataw orim*

at me	**agam**
	ugum
at you (singular)	**agat**
	ugut
at him	**aige**
	egge
at her	**aice**
	ekee
at us	**againn**
	ugeen
at you (plural)	**agaibh**
	ugiv
at them	**acu**
	akoo

Note the use of the preposition **ag** (at) to imply possession of a thing, e.g. **tá Gaeilge agam** (I have Irish, literally 'Irish is at me'), or **tá cóta agam** (I have a coat).

Days of the week

Sunday	**Dé Domhnaigh**
	je downee
Monday	**Dé Luain**
	je looin
Tuesday	**Dé Máirt**
	je martch
Wednesday	**Dé Céadaoin**
	je kaydeen
Thursday	**Déardaoin**
	jeyrdeen
Friday	**Dé hAoine**
	je haynya
Saturday	**Dé Sathairn**
	je saharn
yesterday	**inné**
	inyay
today	**inniu**
	inyoo
tomorrow	**amárach**
	amawrakh
tonight	**anocht**
	anukht

tomorrow night	**oíche amárach** *eeha amawrakh*
last night	**aréir** *areyr*
where were you last night?	**cá raibh tú aréir?** *ka row too areyr*
I was in the pub	**bhí mé sa teach tábhairne** *vee may sa chakh tawarnya*
where are we going tomorrow?	**cá bhfuilimid ag dul amárach?** *ka'l mij eg dul amawrakh*
we are going to the beach	**táimid ag dul go dtí an trá** *tamij eg dul gujee in tra*
what day is it?	**cad é an lá inniu?** *kajay in law inyoo*
it's Friday	**inniu an Aoine** *inyoo an aynya*
what's the matter?	**cad é tá cearr?** *kajay taw kyarr*
nothing	**rud ar bith** *rud air bih*
help yourself to the milk	**tarraing ort an bainne** *tarring urt a banya*
it cannot be helped	**níl neart air** *neeil nyart air*
I have no choice	**níl an dara suí sa bhuaile agam** *neeil in dara see sa woolya ugum*

(Literally, this means, 'I haven't a second place in the mountain pasture'!)

An Irish proverb

in the land of the blind the one-eyed man is king	**i dtír na ndall is rí fear na leathshúile** *i jeer na nall iss ree far na lyah-hoola*

Parts of the body

head	**ceann** *kyunn*
hair	**gruaig** *grooag* (U), *grooig* (C, M)
your hair	**do chuid gruaige** *du khuj grooiga*
the face	**an aghaidh** *in I*
eye	**súil** *sooil*
the eyes	**na súile** *na sooila*
the nose	**an tsrón** *in troan*
the mouth	**an béal** *in bell*
chin	**smig** *smig*
ear	**cluas** *klooas*
forehead	**éadan** *eydin*
tooth	**fiacail** *feeakal*
teeth	**fiacla** *feeakla*
cheek	**leiceann** *lekann*
throat	**scornach** *skornakh*
shoulder	**gualainn** *gooalann*
shoulder-blade	**slinneán** *slinyaun*
arm	**sciathán** *skeeahan*
elbow	**uillinn** *ilyinn*
hand	**lámh** *lauw (or lauv)*
finger	**méar** *meyr*
the fingers	**na méara** *na meyra*

chest	**brollach** (and **cliabh**)
	brulakh (and *kleeoow*)
stomach	**goile**
	gila
belly	**bolg**
	bulig
waist	**coim**
	kim
leg	**cos** (and **cois**)
	kuss (and *kush*)
thigh	**más**
	mass
knee	**glúin**
	glooin
calf	**colpa**
	kullepa
ankle	**murnán**
	murnaun

Regular Verbs

stand	**seas**
	shass

Present tense:

I stand	**seasaim**
	shassim
you stand	**seasann tú**
	shassan too
he/she stands	**seasann sé/sí**
	shassan shay/shee
we stand	**seasaimid**
	shassimij
you stand (pl.)	**seasann sibh**
	shassan shiv
they stand	**seasann siad**
	shassan sheead

Past tense:

I stood	**sheas mé**
	hass may
you stood	**sheas tú**
	hass too
he/she stood	**sheas sé/sí**
	hass shay/shee

we stood	**sheasamar**
	hassamar
you (pl.) stood	**sheas sibh**
	hass shiv
they stood	**sheas siad**
	hass sheead

Future tense:

I stand	**seasfaidh mé**
	shass-hee may
you will stand	**seasfaidh tú**
	shass-hee too
he/she will stand	**seasfaidh sé/sí**
	shass-hee shay/shee
we shall stand	**seasfaimid**
	hass-heemij
you will stand (pl.)	**seasfaidh sibh**
	shass-hee shiv
they will stand	**seasfaidh siad**
	shass-hee sheead

Some regular verbs:

move	**bog**
	bug
twist	**cas**
	kass
sell	**díol**
	jeel
praise	**mol**
	mul
take	**glac**
	glak
follow	**lean**
	lan
stop	**stad**
	stad
swim	**snámh**
	snauw (U), *snauv* (C, M)
write	**scríobh**
	skrioo (U), *skreev* (C, M)
clean	**glan**
	glan
fill	**líon**
	leen

raise, build, or take	**tóg**
	taug

The Calendar

month	**mí**
	mee
January	**Mí Eanáir**
	mee annar
February	**Mí Feabhra**
	mee fyouwra
March	**Márta**
	marta
April	**Aibreán**
	abran
May	**Mí na Bealtaine**
	mee na baltanya
June	**Meitheamh**
	mehoow
July	**Mí lúil**
	mee yooil
August	**Mí Lúnasa**
	mee loonassa
September	**Meán Fómhair**
	man fowar
October	**Deireadh Fómhair**
	jerroo fowar
November	**Mí na Samhna**
	mee na souwna
December	**Mí na Nollag**
	mee na nullag

There are numerous alternatives to the names given above; the word **mí** may precede the name, be omitted, or used with the article **an**. There are many variaions, among them:

February	**Mí na bhFaoilleach**
	mee na waeelyakh
June	**Mí mheáin an tSamh-raidh**
	mee van a towree
June	**Mí na Féile Eoin**
	mee na feyla owen

July   **Mí na Súl Buí**
mee na sool bwee

Negative of regular verbs:

stand   **seas**
shass

Present:
I move   **bogaim**
bugim

I do not move   **ní bhogaim**
nee wugim

Past:
I moved   **bhog mé**
wug may

I did not move   **níor bhog mé**
neer wug may

Future:
I shall move   **bogfaidh mé**
bug-hee may

I shall not move   **ní bhogfaidh mé**
nee wug-hee may

To ask a question:

Place *an* before the verb in the present and future tenses, and *ar* in the past tense. For example:

break   **bris**
brish

do they break?   **an mbriseann siad?**
un mrishin sheead

will they break?   **an mbrisfidh siad?**
un mrish-hee sheead

did they break?   **ar bhris siad?**
air vrish sheead

did you break it?   **ar bhris tú é?**
air vrish too ay

Note that *b* is eclipsed by *an*, i.e. *mb* and *b* is not heard, *ar* aspirates the *b*, and it now sounds like *v* (or *w* if used with a broad vowel).

When a verb begins with a vowel or with *f*, it is prefixed by *d* in the past tense. For example:

I drink	**ólaim**
	aulim
I drank	**d'ól mé**
	daul may
he waits	**fanann sé**
	fanin shay
he waited	**d'fhan sé**
	dan shay

Telling the time

what time is it?	**cad é an t-am e?**
	kaday in tam
it is one o'clock	**tá sé a haon a chlog**
	taw shay a hayn a khlug
it is two o'clock	**tá sé a dó a chlog**
	taw shay a dau a khlug
it is half past three	**tá sé leath tar éis a trí**
	taw shay lyah tar esh a tree
after	**tar éis** (C, M) **i ndiaidh** (U)
	tar esh/in yay
it is half past four	**tá sé leath i ndiaidh** (or, **tar éis**) **a ceathair**
	taw shay lyah in yay a kehar
it is a quarter past five	**tá sé ceathrú tar éis a cúig**
	taw shay kehroo tar esh a kuig
it is a quarter to six	**tá sé ceathrú go dtí a sé**
	taw shay kehroo go jee a shay
it is twenty past seven	**tá sé fiche i ndiaidh a seacht**
	taw shay fiha in yay a shakht

it is twenty to eight	**tá sé fiche go dtí a hocht**
	taw shay fiha gu jee a hukht

Note the dialectal differences with *after*: **i ndiaidh** is more common in Ulster, while **tar éis** is used in Munster and Connacht.

Possessive adjectives:

The possessive pronouns, *mine, yours, his, her, our, their,* do not exist as such in Irish, but the possessive adjective can be used to express the same concept:

my coat	**mo chóta**
	mu khota
your coat	**do chóta**
	du khota
his coat	**a chóta**
	a khota
her coat	**a cóta**
	a kota
our coat	**ár gcóta**
	arr gota
your (pl.) coat	**bhur gcóta**
	wur gota
their coat	**a gcóta**
	a gota

Note that **mo** (my), **do** (your), **a** (his), all aspirate the following noun (provided it begins with a consonant capable of being aspirated). **a** (her), neither aspirates nor eclipses the following noun but prefixes an *h* to any following vowel, e.g. **a hathair** (her father). **a** (their), **bhur** (your *pl.*), **ar** (our) all eclipse the following noun where possible. For example:

their father	**a n-athair**
	a nahar
our father	**ár n-athair**
	arr nahar
your father	**bhur n-athair**
	wur nahar

Conversation

Talking is a popular pastime in Ireland. Here are some terms relating to the art of conversation:

conversation	**comhrá** *kowra*
you are talking nonsense	**tá tú ag glagaireacht** *taw too eg glagarakht*
speaking	**ag labhairt** *eg lowartch*
chattering	**geabaireacht** *gyabarakht*
whisper	**cogar** *kugar*
he whispered to me	**chuir se cogar i mo chluais** *khur shay kugar i mu khlooish*
gossip	**ráfla** *raffla*
I heard a rumour	**chuala me ráfla** *hula may raffla*
tongue-twister	**rabhlóg** *rouwlog*
shout	**scairt** *skartch*
raving	**rámhaille** *rowalya*
scream	**scread** *skrad*
yelling	**béicíl** *beykeel*
he let out a scream	**lig sé beic as** *lig shay beyk ass*
complain	**gearán/clamhsán** *gyaraun/klouwsaun*
backbiting	**cúlchaint** *koolkhantch*
eavesdrop	**cúléist** *kooleysht*
eavesdropper	**cúléisteoir** *kooleyshtyor*
boasting	**ag maíomh** *eg mweeoo*
narrative	**scéalaíocht** *skeyleeakht*

news	**scéala**
	skeyla
story	**scéal**
	skeyl
argument	**argóint**
	arigointch
I saw a good film last night	**chonaic me scannán maith aréir**
	hanik may skanan maith areyr
there is a good film on the television tonight	**tá scannán maith ar an teilifís anocht**
	taw skanan maith air in tellefish anukht

Accomodation and Hotels

hotel	**teach ósta/óstlann**
	chack austa/austlan
we are staying at a hotel	**táimid ag fanacht i dteach ósta**
	tawmij a fanakht i jach usta
send the maid up	**cuir an cailín aimsire aníos chugainn**
	kur in kaleen imshera aneeas hugeen
is there a bathroom on this floor?	**an bhfuil seomra folchtha or an urlár seo?**
	un will shumra fulka air in urlar shaw
towel	**tuáille**
	too-oilya
soap	**gallúnach**
	galoonakh

The churches frequently hold services in Irish when and where appropriate. Anyone attending these should try to obtain the printed texts to be used, which are often readily available.

the church	**an Eaglais**
	in aglish
chapel	**teach an phobail**
	chakh a fubal
Mass	**aifreann**
	affrin
church service	**seirbhís eaglasta**
	shervish aglasta
The Church of Ireland	**Eaglais na hÉireann**
	aglish na heyrann
the priest	**an sagart**
	in saggart
the minister	**an ministir**
	in minishter

---

do you have any rooms free?	**an bhfuil aon seomra saor agat?**
	un will aen shomrah seer ugut?
I'd like a room...	**ba mhaith liom seomra...**
	bah waih lyum shom-rah...
with a double bed	**le leaba dhúbailte**
	leh lyaba dhoobal-tche
with twin beds	**le dhá leaba**
	leh ghaa lyabah
with a bathroom	**le seomra folctha**
	leh shomrah folk-ha
with a nice view	**le radharc deas**
	leh rowark jass
at the front	**ag an tosach**
	eg un tussahh
at the back	**ar chúl**
	er khool
we will be staying...	**beimid ag fanacht...**
	bay mij eg fanakht
overnight	**thar oíche**
	har eeha
a couple of days	**cúpla lá**
	koopla la
a week	**ar feadh seachtaine**
	er fow shahhtenya

a fortnight	**ar feadh coicíse**
	er fow kukisha
perhaps	**b'fhéidir**
	bay-jer
may I see the room	**an féidir liom an seomra a fheiceáil**
	un fey jer lyum a shom-rah ah ekoyl
I don't like it	**ní maith liom é**
	nee maih lyum ay
it is...	**tá sé...**
	tau shay
too small	**ró bheag**
	roh vug
too cold	**ró fhuar**
	roh uar
too dark	**ró dhorcha**
	roh ghor ahha
too noisy	**ró challánach**
	roh hhallanahh
too dirty	**ró shalach**
	roh halakh
give me	**tabhair dom**
	tawer dum
give me a bigger room	**tabhair dom seomra níos mó**
	tawer dum shomrah nees mo

Food

bread	**arán**
	arann
toast	**arán rósta**
	arann rawsta
brown bread	**arán donn**
	arann dunn
potato bread	**arán prátí**
	arann pratee
wheaten bread	**arán cruithneachta**
	arann krihnakhta
oaten bread	**arán coirce**
	arann kur-ka
salt	**salann**
	salan

pepper	**piobar**
	pibbar
garlic	**gairleog**
	garlyog
sea salt	**salann sáile**
	salan soyl-a
meat	**feoil**
	fyawil
mutton	**caoireoil**
	keeryawil
bacon	**bagún**
	bagoon
pork	**muiceoil**
	mukyawil
beef	**feoil mhairt**
	fyawil wartch
sausage	**ispín**
	ishpeen
sausages	**ispíní**
	ishpeenee
potatoes	**prátaí**
	pratee

Garlic was never very popular in Irish cooking, but still is well known and widely available. It was once fed to cattle and other livestock to protect them from disease as its medical properties were highly regarded by country people. Its main use among the Irish population, therefore, was medicinal. It is still taken as a medicine in some areas during epidemics of cold and 'flu.

sugar	**siúcra**
	shookra
egg	**ubh**
	iv
eggs	**uibheacha**
	ivakha
boiled egg	**ubh bhruite**
	iv vritcha
fried eggs	**uibheacha friochta**
	ivakha frikhta

scrambled eggs	**uibheacha scrofa** *ivakha skrufa*
a raw egg	**ubh amh** *iv auw*
tea	**tae** *tay*
coffee	**caife** *kafee*
milk	**bainne** *banya*
goat's milk	**bainne gabhair** *banya gowayr*
buttermilk	**bláthach** *bla-akh*
cheese	**cáis** (C, M), **cáise** (U) *kaash* (C,M), *kaashee* (U)
butter	**im** *imm*
home-made butter	**im baile** *im bala*
fish	**iasc** (*plural:* **éisc**) *eeask (ayshk)*
trout	**breac** (*plural:* **bric**) *brak (brik)*
sea trout	**brak geal** *brak gyal*
salmon	**bradán** (pl: **bradáin**) *braddan (bradoin)*
mackerel	**murlas** *murlass*
cod	**trosc** *trusk*
herrings	**scadán** *skaddan*
mussels	**sliogáin dhubha** *sligoyn goow-a*
or	**diúilicíní** *joolikeenee*
oysters	**oisrí** *ushree*
crab	**portán** *purtann*
lobster	**gliomach** *glimmakh*
chicken	**sicín** *shikeen*

soup	**anraith**
	anreeh
vegetable soup	**anraith glasraí**
	anreeh glassree
onions	**oinniúin**
	unyoowin
sauce	**anlann**
	annlann

An Irish saying:

Hunger is good sauce	**Is maith an t-anlann an t-ocras**
	iss moih an tannlann un tukrass

---

tomatoes	**trátaí**
	traatee
beans	**pónairí**
	pownaree
carrot	**meacan dearg**
	mekan jareg
beetroot	**biatas**
	beeatass
parsnips	**meacan bán**
	mekan bawn

Another regular verb:

dwell	**cónaigh**
	konee

Present tense:

I dwell	**cónaím**
	koneeim
you dwell	**cónaíonn tú**
	koneean too
he/she dwells	**cónaíonn sé/sí**
	koneean shay/shee
we dwell	**cónaímid**
	koneeimij
you dwell	**cónaíonn sibh**
	koneean shiv
they dwell	**cónaíonn siad**
	koneean sheead

Past tense:

I dwelt	**chónaigh mé** *khonee may*
you dwelt	**chónaigh tú** *khonee too*
he/she dwelt	**chónaigh sé/sí** *khonee shay/shee*
we dwelt	**chónaíomar** *khoneeamar*
you dwelt	**chónaigh sibh** *khonee shiv*
they dwelt	**chónaigh siad** *khonee sheead*

Future tense:

I shall dwell	**cónóidh mé** *kono-ee may*
you will dwell	**cónóidh tú** *kono-ee too*
he/she will dwell	**cónóidh sé/sí** *kono-ee shay/shee*
we shall dwell	**cónóimid** *kono-eemij*
you will dwell	**cónóidh sibh** *kono-ee shiv*
they will dwell	**cónóidh siad** *kono-ee sheead*

The following are similarly conjugated:

buy	**ceannaigh** *kyanee*
ask	**fiafraigh** *feefree*
search	**cuardaigh** *kooardee*
arrange	**socraigh** *sukree*
begin	**tosaigh** *tusee*
examine	**scrúdaigh** *skroodee*
paint	**dathaigh** *dahee*
satisfy	**sásaigh** *sausee*
cover	**clúdaigh** *kloodee*

protect	**cumhdaigh** *koowdoo*

I prefer	**is fearr liom** *iss farr lyum*
I prefer tea to coffee	**is fearr liom tae ná caife** *iss farr lyum tay na kafee*
I don't like carrots	**ní maith liom meacan dearg** *nee moih lyum mekan jareg*
I like potatoes	**is maith liom prátaí** *iss moih lyum pratee*
do you like milk?	**an maith leat bainne?** *un moih lyat banya*
yes, I do, but I prefer cream	**is maith, ach is fearr liom uachtar** *iss moih akh iss farr lyum ooakhter*
which do you prefer, tea or coffee?	**cé acu is fearr leat: tae nó caife?** *kay akoo iss farr lyat tay no kafee*
would you prefer coffee?	**arbh fhearr leat caife?** *airiv arr lyat kafee*
yes, I would	**b'fhearr** *barr*
would you like more?	**ar mhaith leat tuilleadh?** *air woih lyat chilyoo*
no, thank you	**níor mhaith, go raibh maith agat** *neer woih gurra moih ugut*
she prefers carrots to parsnips	**Is fearr léi meacan dearg ná meacan bán** *iss farr layhe mekan jareg na mekan bawn*
pass me the salt please	**chuir chugam an sal-ann le do thoil** *khur hugim un salan le du huyl*

with me	**liom**
	lyum
with you	**leat**
	lyat
with him	**leis**
	laysh
with her	**léi**
	layhe
with us	**linn**
	ling
with you	**libh**
	liv
with them	**leo**
	law

I would like some bread	**ba mhaith liom giota aráin**
	bu woih lyum gita aroin
do you take sugar?	**an ólann tú siúcra?**
	un awlin too shookra
I do/I don't	**ólaim/ní ólaim**
	awlim/nee awlim
(yes) I am	**tá**
	taw
(no) I am not	**níl**
	nee-il

There is no word for *yes* or *no* in Irish as in English. One simply uses the positive or negative form of the verb used in the question, as in the examples above.

the trout is very tasty	**tá an breac an-bhlasta**
	taw un brak ann-vlasta
the salmon is tasty too	**tá an bradán blasta freisin**
	taw un braddan blasta freshin
have you enough?	**an bhfuil go leor agat?**
	un will gu lyowr ugut

I have had enough	**tá mo sháith agam**
	taw mu hlh ugum
thank you	**go raibh maith agat**
	gurra moih ugut
please	**le do thoil**
	le du huyl
don't mention it	**ná habair é**
	na habber ay
is there any more fish?	**an bhfuil tuilleadh éisc ann?**
	un will tilyoo ayshk unn
red wine	**fíon dearg**
	feen jareg
white wine	**fíon bán**
	feen bawn
cutlery	**sceanra**
	skyanra
do you have…?	**an bhfuil…agat?**
	un will…ugut
I am hungry	**tá ocras orm**
	taw ukrass uram

---

on me	**orm**
	uram
on you	**ort**
	urt
on him	**air**
	air
on her	**uirthi**
	urhee
on us	**orainn**
	ureen
on you	**oraibh**
	uriv
on them	**orthu**
	urha

---

what do you recommend?	**cad é a mholann tú**
	kajay a wullen too
there is too much salt in it	**ta barraíocht salainn ann**
	taw bareeakht saloin ann

a meal	**béile**
	beyla
meals	**béilí**
	beylee
dinner	**dinnéar**
	dinyayr
breakfast	**bricfeasta**
	brikfesta
lunch	**lón**
	loan
restaurant	**teach itheacháin/ proinnteach**
	chakh ihakhoin/ princhakh

Travel

car	**carr**
	karr
coach	**cóiste**
	koshtcha
aeroplane	**eitleán**
	etchilan
ship	**long**
	lung
boat	**bád**
	bawd
bicycle	**rothar**
	ruhar
driving	**ag tiomáint**
	a tchumantch
driving a car	**ag tiomáint cairr**
	a tchumantch ka-yr
driver	**tiománaí**
	tchumanee
who is the driver?	**cé hé an tiománaí?**
	kay hay in tchumanee
(the) road	**(an) bothar**
	in bowhar
throroughfare (or route)	**bealach**
	balakh
flying	**ag eitilt**
	eg etchiltch
flight	**eitilt**
	etchiltch

airport	**aerfort** *airfurt*
how do you get to the airport from here?	**cad é an bealach go dtí an t-aerfort as seo?** *kajay in balakh gujee in tairfurt ass shau*
landing (by ship)	**teacht i dtír** *chakht i jeer*
landing (by plane)	**(ag) tuirlingt** *turlingtch*
I came by plane	**tháinig mé ar an eitleán** *hanig may air in etchilan*
runway	**rúidbhealach** *rooj-valakh*
the plane landed on the runway	**thuirling an t-eitleán ar an rúidbhealach** *hurling in tetchilan air in rooj-valakh*
jetplane	**scairdeitleán** *skarj-etchilan*
crossroads	**crosbhóthar** *krusswowhar*
a trip	**turas** *turiss*
a walk	**siúlóid** *shooloyj*
walking	**ag siúl** *eg shool*
going for a walk	**dul ar siúlóid** *dul air shooloyj*
rambling	**ag spaisteoireacht** *a spashchorakht*
will you take me to the station please?	**an dtabharfaidh tú chuig an stáisiún mé, le do thoil** *in dawrhee too hig in stashoon may, le du huyl*
what is the fare?	**cád é an táille?** *kajay in tal-ya*
two pounds	**dhá phunt** *gaw funt*

where is the booking office?	**cá bhfuil an oifig ticéad?**
	ka'l in ifig chikeyd
enquiries office	**oifig faisnéise**
	ifig fashnesha
platform three	**ardán a trí**
	ardan a tree
luggage	**bagáiste**
	bagoishta
waiting room	**feithealann**
	fehalann
where do you get the train to Dublin?	**cá bhfaigheann tú an traein go Baile Átha Cliath?**
	ka wlyen too in treyn gu bala kleea
when is the next train?	**cá huair a bheidh an chéad traein eile ann?**
	ka hoor a bay in kheydt reyn ella unn
the first train	**an chéad traein**
	in kheyd treyn
the next train	**an chéad traein eile**
	in kheyd treyn ella
the last train	**an traein dheireanach**
	in treyn yeranakh

Most main cities and towns in Ireland can be reached by an arterial rail network with its centre in Dublin, otherwise the provincial bus service can be used. The latter primarily serves rural areas, and short journeys by bus through Irish-speaking districts provide useful opportunities for hearing the language spoken.

---

does the train stop at Athlone?	**an stadann an traein ag Áth Luain?**
	un staden in treyn eg ah looin
yes (it does stop)	**stadann**
	staden
no (it does not stop)	**ní stadann**
	nee staden

what is the quickest way to get to Galway?	**cad é an bealach is giorra go Gaillimh?**
	kajay in balakh iss gyurra gu galyiv
I walked to the house	**shiúil mé go dtí an teach**
	hyooil may gujee in chakh
where is the beach?	**cá bhfuil an trá?**
	ka'l in traw
it's down there	**tá thíos ansin**
	taw hees unshin
is it far?	**an bhfuil sé i bhfad?**
	un will shay i wad
yes, it is two miles	**tá, tá sé dhá mhíle slí**
	taw, taw shay gaw veela slee
how did you get here?	**cén bealach a tháimig tú?**
	keyen balakh a hanig too
I came over the hill	**tháinig mé thar an chnoc**
	hanig may har a kh-nuk
I took a shortcut	**ghearr mé an t-aicearra**
	yar may in tekera
the sea-shore	**an cladach**
	in kladakh
the beach	**an trá**
	in traw (C, M) in trl (U)
the sea	**an fharraige**
	in arriga
sailing	**ag seoladh**
	eg shawloo
sailing boat	**bád seolta**
	bawd shawlta
lake	**loch**
	lokh
mountain	**sliabh**
	sleev (C, M) sleeoo (U)
the mountains	**na sléibhte**
	na slevtche
hill	**cnoc**
	k-nuk (C, M) kruk (U)

the hills	**na cnoic**
	na k-nik (C, M) na krik (U)
a beautiful view	**radharc álainn**
	rawark auleen
sunset	**luí gréine**
	lee greynya
the sun	**an ghrian**
	in ghreean
beautiful	**álainn** (or **go hálainn**)
	auleen (gu hauleen)
it is beautiful	**tá sé go hálainn**
	taw shay gu hauleen
is there anything to see around here?	**an bhfuil rud ar bith le feiceáil thart anseo?**
	un will rud er bih le fekoil hart unshaw
yes, a lot	**tá, cuid mhór**
	taw, kuj wore
for example	**mar shampla**
	mar hampla
there is a castle near this place	**tá caisleán in aice leis an áit seo**
	taw kashlan in eka lesh in Itch shaw
a standing stone	**gallán** (or **liagán**)
	galawn (leeagawn)
a rath	**ráth**
	rah
monastery	**mainistir**
	manishter
round tower	**túr cruinn**
	toor krin
museum	**iarsmalan** (or **músaem**)
	eersmalan (moosaym)
archaeology	**seandálaíocht**
	shandaleeakht
archaeological remains	**iarsmaí seandálaíochta**
	eersmee shandaleeakhta

Many types of archaeological survivals can be found all over Ireland. Forts, souterrains, crannogs, towers, megalithic tombs, standing stones, stone circles, burial mounds and all manner of interesting antiquities literally dot the countryside. They are easily found, especially on O.S. maps, and information about them is readily available (see, for example, *Outings in Ireland* by Hugh Oram, Appletree Press, 1982).

---

up in the mountains	**thuas sna sléibhte** *hooass sna slevtcha*
down in the glen	**thíos sa ghleann** *heess sa ghlann*
among the trees	**i measc na gcrann** *i mask na gran*
the leaves on the trees	**na duilleoga ar na crainn** *na dilyoga air na krin*
a bird in the sky	**éan thuas sa spéir** *eyan hooass sa speyr*
out on the lake	**amuigh ar an loch** *amwee air in lokh*
are there many fish in the river?	**an bhfuil mórán iasc san abhainn?** *un will moran eeask san owen*
I don't know	**níl a fhios agam** *neeil'iss ugum*

---

wonderful	**go hiontach** *gu heentakh*
impressive	**suntasach** *suntasakh*
peaceful	**suaimhneach** *sooivnyakh*
superb	**ar fheabhas** *air owas*
strange	**aisteach** *Ishchakh*
quiet	**ciúin** *kyooin*
interesting	**suimiúil** *simiooil*
tremendous	**millteanach** *milchanakh*
ostentatious	**taibhseach** *tIvshakh*

Sports

football	**peil** *pell*
playing football	**ag imirt peile** *eg imertch pella*
where is the ball?	**cá bhfuil an liathróid?** *ka'l in leeahroij*
it is in the long grass	**tá sí san fhéar fada** *taw shee san yeyr fada*
we've lost it	**tá sí caillte againn** *taw shee klltcha ugeen*
a game of football	**cluiche peile** *kliha pella*
who do you think will win?	**cé a bhainfidh an cluiche i do bharúil?** *kay a winhee a kliha i du warooil*
it's hard to tell	**is doiligh a rá** *iss dilee a raw*
it will be a draw	**beidh sé cothrom** *bay shay kuhrum*
team	**foireann** *furann*
the teams	**na foirne** *na furnya*
golf	**galf** *galf*
golf course	**galfchúrsa** *galfkhoorsa*
what were you doing?	**cad é bhí sibh a dhéanamh?** *kaday vee shiv a yanoo*
we were playing golf	**bhímid ag imirt gailf** *veemij eg emertch galf*
can you swim?	**an bhfuil snámh agat?** *un will snouw ugut*
is there a swimming pool near here?	**an bhfuil linn snámha in aice leis seo?** *un will linn snouwa in eka lesh seo*
swimming pool	**linn snámha** *linn snava (C, M),* *snouwa (U)*

the sea is too cold for swimming	**tá an fharraige rófhuar le haghaidh snámha** *taw in ariga rau-oor le hl snouwa*
hurling	**iománaíocht** *umauneeakht*
hurling stick	**camán** *kamaun*

Gaelic football, **peil Ghaelach**, is the most popular Celtic game in Ireland, closely followed by hurling, **iománaíocht**. Hurling is a fast exciting game but can be dangerous if played without training. Protective headgear is now common and serious injury is comparatively rare. **Camógaíocht**, or camogie, is similar to hurling, and played by women.

---

goal	**cúl** *kool*
the referee	**an réiteoir** *in reytchor*
cycling	**rothaíocht** *ruheeakht*
bicycle	**rothar** *ruhar*
wheel	**roth** *ruh*
the brakes	**na coscáin** *na kuskoin*
where can I hire a bike?	**cá háit a bhfuil rothar le fáil ar cíos** *ka hltch a will ruhar le foil air khees*
I have a puncture	**tá poll sa roth agam** *taw pul sa ruh ugum*
pedal	**troitheán** *treehan*
there are too many hills	**tá barraíocht cnoc ann** *taw bareakht kruk unn*
let's go for a walk	**téimis amach ar shiúlóid** *tcheyimish amakh air hyooloij*

climbing	**dreapadóireacht** *drapadorakht*
sailing	**ag seoladh** *eg shauloo*
sailing boat	**bád seoil** *bawd shawil*
hooker	**pucan** *pukawn*
sail	**seol** *shaul*
mast	**crann** *kran*
the rudder	**an stiúir** *in styoor*
there is a good wind for sailing today	**tá gaoth mhaith sheolta ann inniu** *taw gee woih hyawlta unn inyoo*
horse riding	**marcaíocht** *markeeakht*
horse	**capall** *kapal*
saddle	**diallait** *jeealitch*
my horse has no saddle	**níl diallait ar mo chapall** *neeil jeealitch air mu khapal*
sun-bathing	**ag déanamh bolg le gréin** *eg janoo bulig le greyn*
sunny weather	**aimsir ghréine** *Imsher ghreynya*
fine weather	**aimsir mhaith** *Imsher woih*

Drinking

in the pub	**sa teach tábhairne** *sa chakh tawarnya*
a drink	**deoch** *jukh*
drinking	**ag ól** *eg aul*
what would you like to drink?	**cad é ba mhaith leat le hól?** *kaday ba mhaith leat le haul*

I would like a glass of beer	**ba mhaith liom gloine leanna** *bu woih lyum glinya lanna*
beer	**leann/beoir** *lann/byor*
a pint of beer	**pionta leanna** *pinnta lanna*
cider	**fíon úll/ceirtlis** *feen ool/kyertlish*
wine	**fíon** *feen*
vermouth	**fíon mormónta** *feen morimonta*
whiskey	**uisce beatha** *ishka baha*
spirits	**biotáille** *bitoilya*

The word 'whiskey' comes originally from Irish **uisce beatha**, literally 'the water of life'. The word has re-entered the language in some areas as **fuisce** (*fwishka*), more common in Connacht than elsewhere, and **uisce beatha** is still the more common form of the word. **Poitín** (*potcheen*) is the word for home-made whiskey. **Poitín** is made in almost all parts of Ireland, but it has a particularly strong association with Gaeltacht areas. It can be made from potatoes but also from numerous vegetable products, always to a traditional recipe. Its taste tends towards a certain roughness, especially to the unaccustomed drinker, and there are a number of cocktails available. Anything mixed with **poitín** is called a **manglam** (especially in Connemara). **Poitín** must be taken with caution as its effects can be devastating. In any case making it is an offence, with severe penalties! (For a light-hearted history, see *In Praise of Poteen* by John McGuffin, Appletree Press).

---

give me two pints of beer please	**tabhair dom dhá phionta leanna le do thoil** *tawar dum gau finnta lanna, le du hul*

the same again	**an rud céanna arís** *in rud keyna arish*
this is my round	**seo mo sheal** *shaw mu hyall*
or	**seal s' agamsa** *shall sugumsa*
would you like another one?	**ar mhaith leat ceann eile?** *air woih lyat kyunn ella*
yes (I would)	**ba mhaith** *bu woih*
no (I would not)	**níor mhaith** *neer woih*
would you like a cigarette?	**ar mhaith leat toitín?** *air woih lyat tutcheen*
he is drunk	**tá sé ar meisce** *taw shay air meyshka*

There are various degrees of inebriation. Here are the Irish words for a few of them:

drunk	**ar meisce** *air meyshka*
very drunk	**ar deargmheisce** *air jaregveyshka*
quite drunk	**ólta** *aulta*
'blind drunk'	**caoch ólta** *kayokh aulta*
tipsy	**súgach** *soogakh*

have a drink	**bíodh deoch agat** *beeoo jukh ugut*
wine divulges truth (in vino veritas)	**scilidh fíon fírinne** *skilee feen feerinya*
drink it up and don't let it come back	**caith siar é agus ná lig aniar é** *klh sheer ay ugus na lig anyeer ay*
wine is sweet but paying for it is bitter	**is milis fíon, ach is searbh a íoc** *iss milish feen akh iss sharoo a eek*

one for the road	**deoch an dorais** *jukh a darish*
late drinking	**ragairne** *ragarnya*
to go on a spree of revelry and debauchery	**dul chun drabhláis** *dul hun drowlish*
we went on a spree last night	**chuaigh muid ar na canaí aréir** *hooee mij air na kanee areyr*
cheers (health)	**sláinte** *slauntcha*
sober	**stuama** *stooama*
sobriety	**stuaim** *stooim*
do you take an occasional drink?	**an ólann tú corrdheoch?** *un aulan too koryukh*

Games

(he is) playing cards	**ag imirt cartaí** *eg imertch cartee*
hearts	**hart** (pl. **hairt**) *hart* (pl. *hartch*)
diamonds	**muileata** (pl. **muileataí**) *mwilata* (pl. *mwilatee*)
spades	**spéireata** (pl. **spéireataí**) *speyrata* (pl. *speyratee*)
clubs	**triuf** (pl. **triufanna**) *truf* (pl. *trufanna*)
the ace	**an t-aon** *in tayn*
the jack	**an cuireata** *in kurata*
the queen	**an bhanríon** *in wanreean*
the king	**an rí** *in ree*
the king of hearts	**an rí hairt** *in ree hartch*

trump	**mámh**
	maw
a game	**cluiche**
	kliha
twenty fives	**cúig is fiche**
	kooig iss fiha
chess	**ficheall**
	fihall
draughts	**táiplis**
	taplish
backgammon	**táiplis mhór**
	taplish wore
chess-board	**clár fichille**
	klar fihilya
chess pieces	**foireann fichille**
	furan fihilya
pawn	**giolla**
	(or **ceithearnach**)
	gilla (or *kehernakh*)
the king	**an rí**
	in ree
the queen	**an bhanríon**
	in wanreean
the bishop	**an tEaspag**
	in chaspug
the knight	**an ridire**
	in rijera
the rook	**an caisleán**
	in kashlan
check	**sáinn**
	slnn
in check	**i sáinn**
	i slnn
checkmate	**marbhsháinn**
	maroohlnn
stalemate	**leamhsháinn**
	lyouwhlnn

Chess, backgammon and similar board games
have been played in Ireland since pre-christian
times. They are referred to in the sagas and folk-
tales and there is nearly always some ritual or
allegorical purpose attached to them. Proficiency
at chess was also reputed to be a requirement of
the ancient warrior caste, the *Fianna*.

Fishing

fishing	**iascaireacht** *eeaskarakht*
I went fishing	**chuaigh mé a iascair- eacht** *khoowee may a eeas- karakht*
how is the fishing here?	**cad é mar atá an iascaireacht anseo?** *kajay mar ataw in eeas- karakht unshaw*
it is good	**tá go maith** *taw gu moih*
it is bad	**tá go dona** *taw gu dunna*
it is fairly good	**tá sé go measartha** *taw shay gu massarha*
fishing rod	**slat iascaireachta** *slat eeaskarakhta*
fishing line	**ruaim** *rooim*
fishing hook	**duán** *dooaun*
waders	**buataisí uisce** *booatishee ishka*
to catch a fish	**iasc a cheapadh** *eeask a khapoo*
I caught a salmon	**mharaigh mé bradán** *waree may braddan*
I didn't catch a thing	**níor mharaigh mé rud ar bith** *neer waree may rud air bih*
bait	**baoite** *bweetcha*
flies	**cuileoga** *kilyoga*
worms	**péisteanna** *peyshtanna*
fly-fishing	**iascaireacht chuil** *eeaskarakht khil*
a fish	**iasc** *eeask*
the fish	**an t-iasc** *in cheeask*

can I fish in this river?	**an bhfuil cead agam iascaireacht a dhéanamh san abhainn seo?**
	un will kad ugum eeaskarakht a yanoo san owen shaw
salmon	**bradán**
	braddan
trout	**breac** (pl. **bric**)
	brak (pl. *brik*)
sea trout	**breac geal**
	brak gyal
sea fishing	**iascaireacht mhara**
	eeaskarakht warra
fisherman	**iascaire**
	eeaskara
going to sea	**dul chun na farraige**
	dul hun na fariga
swimming	**ag snámh**
	ag snauv

When addressing someone in Irish, the vocative case is used. This involves placing a before the person's name and, in some cases, aspirating the first letter. Here are a few examples:

Seán (John)	**'A Sheáin'**
	a hyann
Máire (Mary)	**'A Mháire'**
	a wlra
Cairde (friends)	**'A chairde'**
	a kharja
Fir (men)	**'A fheara'**
	a arra
Pádraig (Patrick)	**'A Phádraig'**
	a fawdrig
Séamas (James)	**'A Shéamais'**
	a heymish
Liam (William)	**'A Liam'**
	a leeam
Bean (woman)	**'A bhean'**
	a van
Tomás (Thomas)	**'A Thomáis'**
	a homish

| 'Be quiet, children' | **'Ciúnas a pháistí'**
kyoonass a fawshtee |

Music

music	**ceol** *kyaul*
do you like music?	**an maith leat an ceol?** *un moih lyat an kyaul*
yes (I do)	**is maith** *iss moih*
no (I don't)	**ní maith** *nee moih*
I don't really care	**is cuma liom** *iss kuma lyum*
I don't mind it	**ní miste liom é** *nee mishtcha lyum ay*
traditional music	**ceol traidisiúnta** *kyaul tradishoonta*
playing music	**ag seinm ceoil** *eg shenyim kyoil*
can you play?	**an féidir leat seinm?** *un feyjer lyat shenyim*
you played it well	**sheinn tú go maith é** *heyn too gu moih ay*
entertainment (musical)	**siamsa** *sheeamsa*
he is playing well	**tá sé ag seinm go maith** *taw shay eg shenyim gu moih*
the fiddle/violin	**an fhidil** *in ijil*
the fiddle is my favourite instrument	**an fhidil an gléas is ansa liom** *in ijil in gless iss ansa lyum*
which is your favourite instrument?	**cén gléas is fearr leat?** *kay akoo gless iss fearr lyat*
a musical instrument	**gléas ceoil** *gless kyoil*

the Irish pipes   **an phíb**
                   in feeb
(Also called *uillean pipes* because they are pumped by a bellows under the arm.)

Scottish bagpipes **píob mhór**
                   peeb wore

piping   **píobaireacht**
                   peebarakht

those pipes are out of tune   **tá an phíob sin as gléas**
                   taw in feeb shin ass gless

accordion   **bosca ceoil**
                   buska kyoil

what sort of tune is that?   **cad é an cineál poirt é sin?**
                   kaday in kinyal portch ay shin

it's a hornpipe   **cornphíopa atá ann**
                   kornfeepa ataw unn

play a jig   **buail suas port**
                   booil sooass purt
(The word **port** can also mean 'a tune'.)

jigs (or tunes)   **poirt**
                   portch

reels   **ríleanna**
                   reelanna

Traditional Irish music is as popular today as ever, and is widely available on records, etc. 'Sessions' of Irish music are common, and there are a number of professional players. Most musicians are amateurs, however, and come from a large cross-section of the population. The music is based on a native 'modal' system which gives it its characteristic flavour. It also has its own system of ornamentation and accents which give it its so-called 'lilt'.

---

drum   **bodhrán**
                   bowran

concertina   **consairtín**
                   kunsarteen

bravo!   **maith thú**
                   moih hoo

song	**amhrán**
	awraun
singer	**amhránaí**
	awraunee
he is a good singer (or player)	**is maith an ceoltóir é**
	iss moih in kyaultor ay
that's a nice song	**sin amhrán deas**
	shin awraun jass
dancing	**rince** (C, M) **damhsa** (U)
	rinka, dowsa
that girl is a fine dancer	**is breá an rinceoir an cailín sin**
	iss braw in rinkyor in kaleenshin
will there be any music tonight?	**an mbeidh aon cheol ann anocht?**
	un may ayn khyaul unn anukht
yes (there will be)	**beidh**
	bay
no (there will not be)	**ní bheidh**
	nee vay
there was a good 'session' in the pub last night	**bhí seisiún maith sa teach tábhairne aréir**
	vee seshoon moih sa chakh tawarnya areyr
there were a lot of musicians playing there	**bhí a lán ceoltóirí ag seinm ansin**
	vee a lawn kyaultoree eg shenyim unshin
how many fiddlers were there?	**cá mhéad fidléir a bhí ann?**
	ka veyd fijiler a vee unn
three fiddlers	**triúr fidléir**
	troor fijiler
no fiddlers	**fidléir ar bith**
	fijiler air bih
tin whistle	**feadóg**
	feejog
flute	**feadóg mhór**
	fadog wore
flute music	**ceol na feadóige**
	kyaul na fadoiga

what did you think of the music?
cad é a shíl tú den cheol?
kajay a heel too din khyaul

I didn't enjoy it
níor thaitin sé liom
neer hatchin shay lyum

it was fine
bhí sé go breá
vee shay gu braw

it was average
bhí sé go measartha
vee shay gu massarha

it was terrible
bhí sé go holc
veeshay gu hulk

sweet music
ceol binn
kyaul binn

harmonious
binn
binn

Shopping

buying things
ag ceannach rudaí
a kyanakh rudee

goods
earraí
arree

supermarket
sármhargadh
sarwaragoo

a good bargain
margadh maith
maragoo moih

you got a good bargain there
fuair tú margadh maith ansin
foor too maragoo moih ansin

what price is it?
cad é an luach atá air?
kajay in luach ata air

how much is it?
cá mhéad sin?
kaveyd shin

it is five pounds
cúig phunt atá air
kooig funt ataw air

it's too dear
tá sé ródhaor
taw shay raugeer

give me something else
tabhair dom rud éigin eile
tawar dum rud eygin ella

show me another one
taispeáin ceann eile dom
tashpan kyunn ella dom

I don't like this one	**ní maith liom an ceann seo**
	nee moih lyum in kyunn shaw
I prefer this one	**is fearr liom an ceann seo**
	iss farr lyum in kyunn shaw
a clothes shop	**siopa éadaí**
	shuppa eydee
where can I buy sweets?	**cá háit arbh fhéidir liom milseáin a cheannach?**
	ka hltch erivejer lyum milshoin a kyanakh
I don't like the colour of it	**ní maith liom an dath atá air**
	nee moih lyum in dah ataw air
what did you buy?	**cad é a cheannaigh tú?**
	kajay a khyanee too
nothing	**rud ar bith**
	rud air bih

The Wind That Shakes the Barley
A selection of Irish Folk-songs

Gareth James

Gareth James has selected over forty well-known Irish folk-songs, plus a number of new songs by contemporary writers. Also included are music and guitar chords. Titles include *As I Roved Out, The Black Velvet Band, The Curragh of Kildare, The Rocky Road to Dublin, The Spanish Lady, Whiskey in the Jar, I'll Tell My Ma, Carrickfergus* and *Goodbye Mursheen Durkin*.

Pocket Tin Whistle Book

Francis McPeake

Francis McPeake's *Pocket Tin Whistle Book* includes a fine collection of forty jigs, reels, slow airs and hornpipes, which the author has transcribed for the tin whistle. Advice is also given on breath control and style, as well as the more complex aspects of ornamentation. Among the tunes are *Father O'Flynn, The Blackthorn Stick, Lannigan's Ball, The Lark in the Morning, Morrison's Jig, The Merry Blacksmith, The Ash Plant* and *The Copper Plate*.